KS1
4–6
Years

Master Maths at Home

Numbers to 100

Scan the QR code to help your child's learning at home.

 | **MATHS** NO PROBLEM! ⊠

mastermathsathome.com

How to use this book

Maths — No Problem! created **Master Maths at Home** to help children develop fluency in the subject and a rich understanding of core concepts.

Key features of the Master Maths at Home books include:

- Carefully designed lessons that provide structure but also allow flexibility in how they're used. For example, some children may want to write numbers, while others might want to trace.

- Speech bubbles containing content designed to spark diverse conversations, with many discussion points that don't have obvious 'right' or 'wrong' answers.

- Rich illustrations that will guide children to a discussion of shapes and units of measurement, allowing them to make connections to the wider world around them.

- Exercises that allow a flexible approach and can be adapted to suit any child's cognitive or functional ability.

- Clearly laid out pages that encourage children to practise a range of higher-order skills.

- A community of friendly and relatable characters who introduce each lesson and come along as your child progresses through the series.

You can see more guidance on how to use these books at **mastermathsathome.com**.

We're excited to share all the ways you can learn maths!

Copyright © 2022 Maths — No Problem!

Maths — No Problem!
mastermathsathome.com
www.mathsnoproblem.com
hello@mathsnoproblem.com

First published in Great Britain in 2022 by
Dorling Kindersley Limited
One Embassy Gardens, 8 Viaduct Gardens, London SW11 7BW
A Penguin Random House Company

The authorised representative in the EEA is Dorling Kindersley
Verlag GmbH. Amulfstr. 124, 80636 Munich, Germany

10 9 8 7 6 5 4 3 2 1
001-327063-Jan/22

A CIP catalogue record for this book is available from the British Library.

ISBN: 978-0-24153-894-4
Printed and bound in China

For the curious
www.dk.com

This book was made with Forest Stewardship Council™ certified paper - one small step in DK's commitment to a sustainable future. For more information go to www.dk.com/our-green-pledge

Acknowledgements
The publisher would like to thank the authors and consultants Andy Psarianos, Judy Hornigold, Adam Gifford and Dr Anne Hermanson.

The Castledown typeface has been used with permission from the Colophon Foundry.

Contents

Ruby   Elliott   Amira   Charles   Lulu   Sam   Oak   Holly   Ravi   Emma   Jacob   Hannah

Counting and writing to 20

Starter

How many cubes does Ravi have?

Example

14

We can join them together to add them up.

I can use a ☐☐☐☐☐. It is called a ten frame.

I can count on from 10. I think it is easier this way.

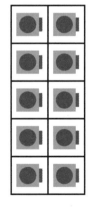

10   11   12   13   14

Ravi has 14 cubes.

1 Count on from 10 and trace the numbers.

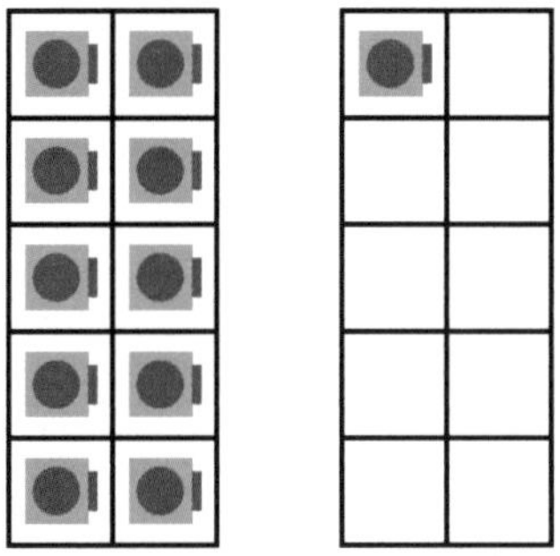

11   eleven

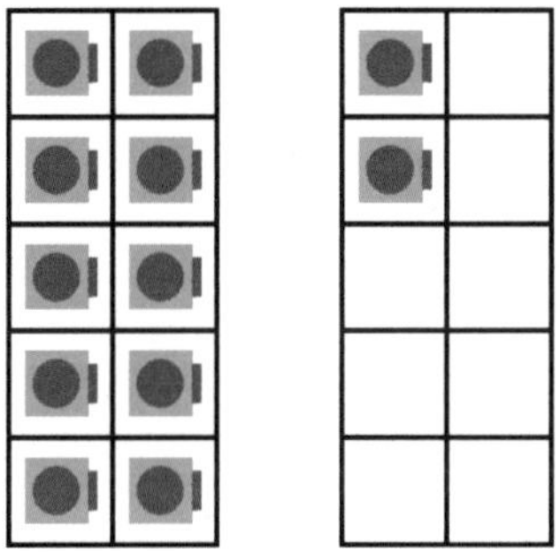

12   twelve

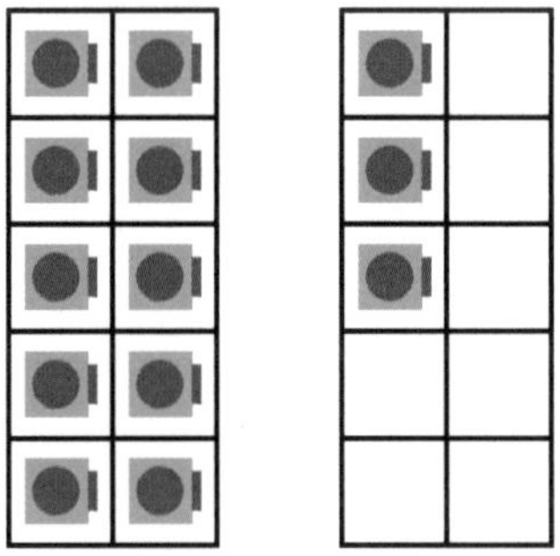

13   thirteen

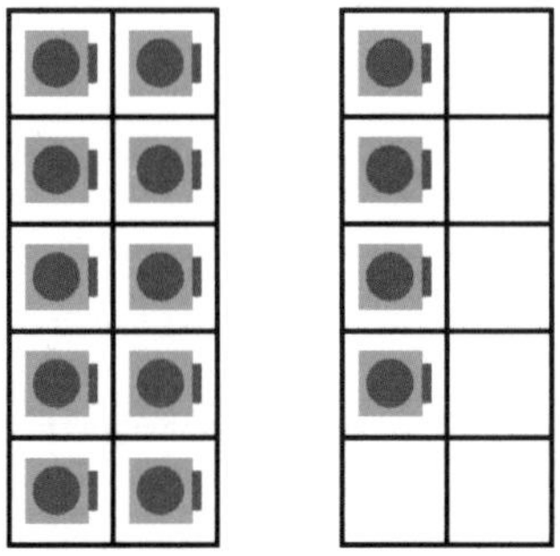

14   fourteen

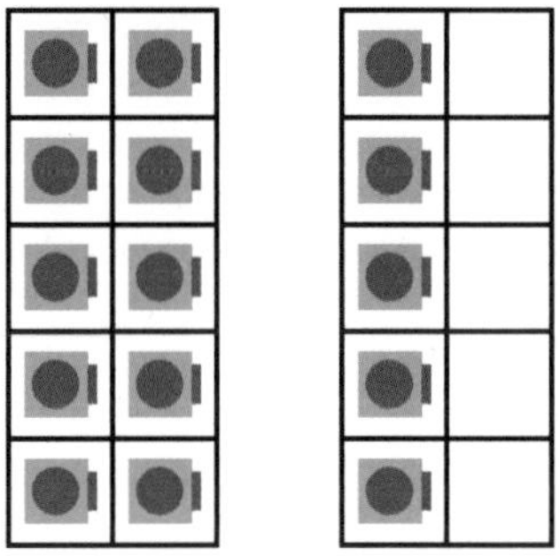

15   fifteen

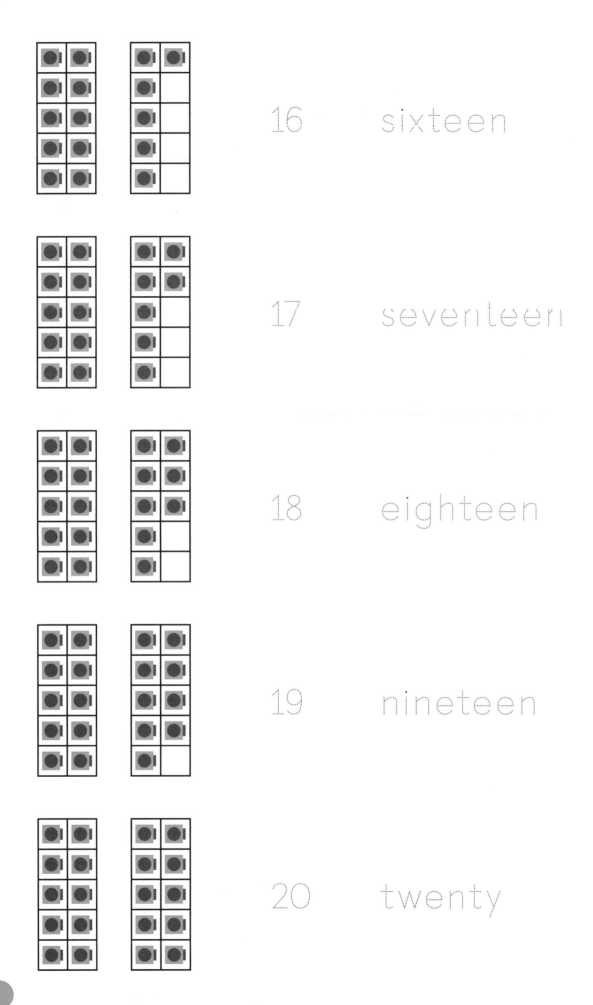

16   sixteen

17   seventeen

18   eighteen

19   nineteen

20   twenty

2 Draw lines to match.

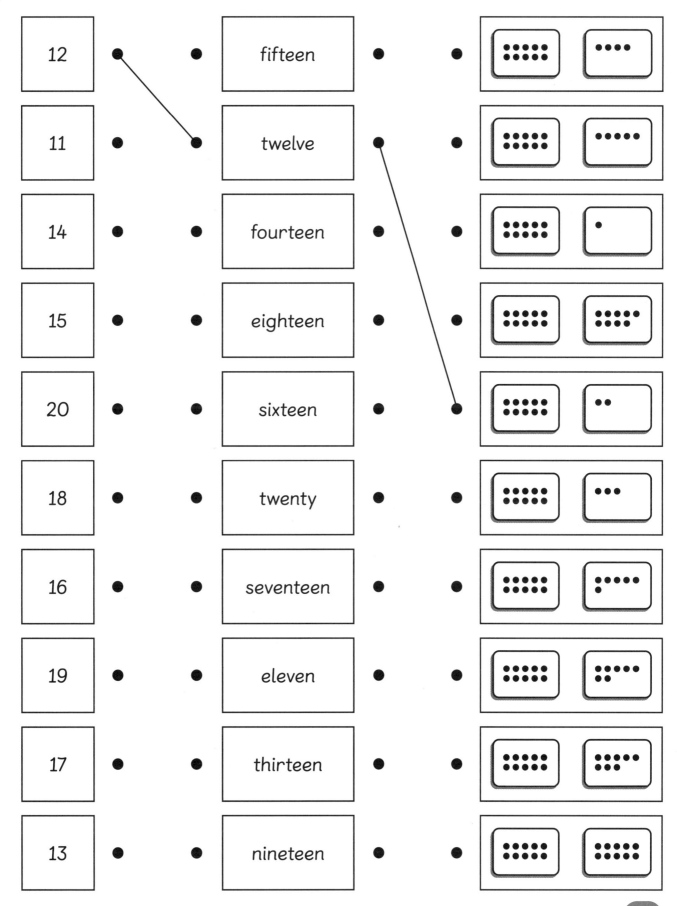

12	fifteen
11	twelve
14	fourteen
15	eighteen
20	sixteen
18	twenty
16	seventeen
19	eleven
17	thirteen
13	nineteen

Comparing and ordering numbers

Starter

The farmer is about to pick his fruit. Which tree has more pieces of fruit? How many more?

Example

Count on from 10 to find out how many lemons there are.

10 lemons

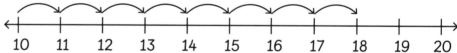

There are 18 lemons in total.

Count on from 10 to find out how many oranges there are.

10 oranges

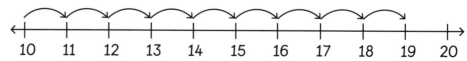

There are 19 oranges in total.

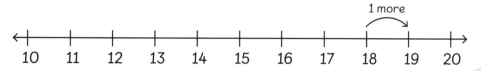

The orange tree has **more** pieces of fruit.
The orange tree has 1 more piece of fruit than the lemon tree.

19 is 1 more than 18.

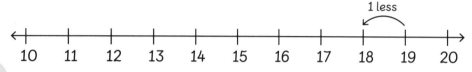

18 is 1 less than 19.

The lemon tree has 1 less piece of fruit than the orange tree.
We can also say that the lemon tree has **fewer** pieces of fruit than the orange tree.

2

16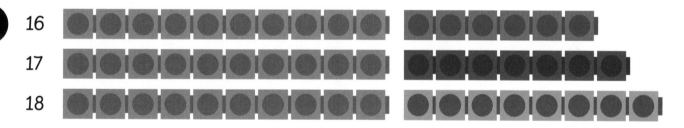
17
18

The smallest number of cubes is 16.
The greatest number of cubes is 18.
17 is 1 more than 16 and 1 less than 18.

We can put the numbers in order from smallest to greatest.
16, 17, 18

We can also put the numbers in order from greatest to smallest.
18, 17, 16

1 Use **more** or **fewer** to fill in the blanks.

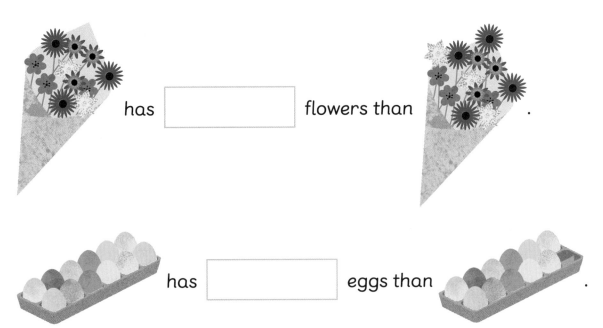

has [   ] flowers than [   ] .

has [   ] eggs than [   ] .

2 (a) Circle the group with more toys.

(b) Circle the group with fewer flowers.

3 Put the numbers in order from smallest to greatest.

(a)

| 13 | 11 | 18 |

☐ ☐ ☐

(b)

| 20 | 14 | 13 |

☐ ☐ ☐

4 Put the numbers in order from greatest to smallest.

(a)

| 15 | 19 | 12 |

☐ ☐ ☐

(b)

| 17 | 12 | 16 |

☐ ☐ ☐

5 Compare 17, 12, and 19.

(a) The smallest number is ☐ .

(b) ☐ is the greatest number.

6 Fill in the blanks.

(a) 12, 11, 10, ☐ , 8, 7

(b) ☐ , 19, 18, 17, 16

(c) ☐ is 1 more than 17.

(d) 14, ☐ , ☐ , 17, 18

(e) ☐ , 17, 18, 19, ☐

(f) ☐ is 1 less than 19.

Ways to add

Starter

Hannah and Sam both brought cupcakes for the party.
How many cupcakes are there in total?

Example

1

Hannah
brought 7 cupcakes.
Sam brought 4 cupcakes.
I can count on from 7.

It's easier to count on
from the greater number.

7   8   9   10   11

I can make 10 to find out how many cupcakes there are in total.

4 can be split into 3 and 1. I can put the 3 with the 7 to make 10.

$$7 + 4 = 10 + 1$$

3   1

There are 11 cupcakes in total.

2

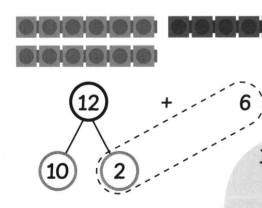

Ravi brought 12 bananas and Holly brought 6 apples.
How many pieces of fruit did they bring in total?

$$12 + 6 = 10 + 8$$

10   2

Ravi and Holly brought 18 pieces of fruit.

I can add the ones to find out how many pieces of fruit there are.
12 is 1 ten and 2 ones.
I can add the 2 ones to the 6 ones.
$$2 + 6 = 8$$
I have 1 ten and 8 ones.

1 Add by counting on. Use the number chart to help you.

1	2	3	4	5	6	7	8	9	10
11	12	13	14	15	16	17	18	19	20

(a) $9 + 3 =$ ⬚

(b) $3 + 8 =$ ⬚

(c) $16 + 2 =$ ⬚

(d) $8 + 4 =$ ⬚

(e) $11 + 5 =$ ⬚

(f) $3 + 17 =$ ⬚

2 Make 10.
Colour the ten frames and fill in the blanks.
The first one is done for you.

(a)

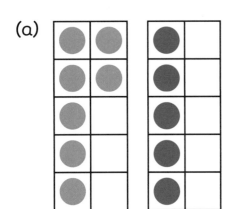 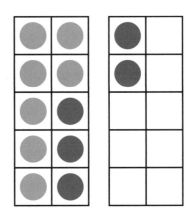

7 + 5 = ⬚ 12

(b)

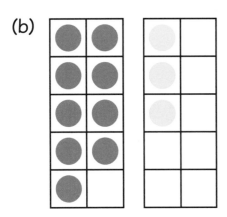 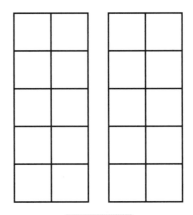

9 + 3 = ⬚

(c)

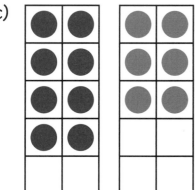 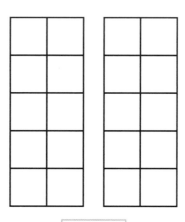

$$8 \quad + \boxed{} \quad = \quad \boxed{}$$

(d)

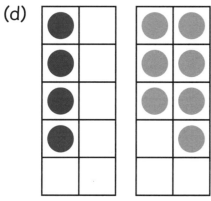 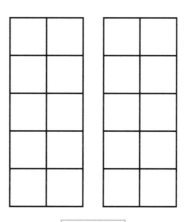

$$\boxed{} \quad + \boxed{} \quad = \quad \boxed{}$$

3 Add the ones, then fill in the blanks.

(a)

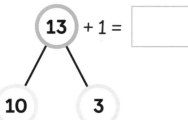

$$13 + 1 = \boxed{}$$

(b) $1 + 12 = \boxed{}$

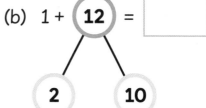

(c)

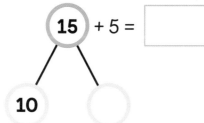

$$15 + 5 = \boxed{}$$

(d) $8 + 12 = \boxed{}$

Ways to subtract

Jacob and Emma plant 16 carrots in the school garden.
The rabbit takes 4 carrots.

How many carrots remain in the ground?

1

I can count back 4 from 16.

I can subtract like this.

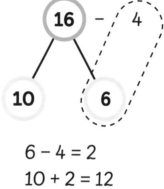

6 – 4 = 2

10 + 2 = 12

There are 12 carrots left.

2

The rabbit comes back and takes 4 more carrots. How many carrots are now left in the ground?

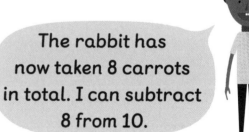

The rabbit has now taken 8 carrots in total. I can subtract 8 from 10.

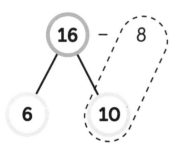

10 – 8 = 2

6 + 2 = 8

There are 8 carrots left.

1 Subtract by counting back. Use the number track to help you.

(a) 15 − 4 = [ ]

| 5 | 6 | 7 | 8 | 9 | 10 | 11 | 12 | 13 | 14 | 15 | 16 | 17 | 18 | 19 | 20 |

(b) 17 − 3 = [ ]

| 5 | 6 | 7 | 8 | 9 | 10 | 11 | 12 | 13 | 14 | 15 | 16 | 17 | 18 | 19 | 20 |

(c) 12 − 6 = [ ]

| 5 | 6 | 7 | 8 | 9 | 10 | 11 | 12 | 13 | 14 | 15 | 16 | 17 | 18 | 19 | 20 |

(d) 14 − 7 = [ ]

| 5 | 6 | 7 | 8 | 9 | 10 | 11 | 12 | 13 | 14 | 15 | 16 | 17 | 18 | 19 | 20 |

2 Subtract from the ones, then fill in the blanks.

(a) 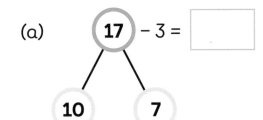 17 − 3 = [ ]

(b) 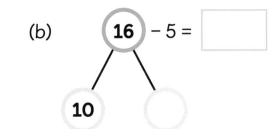 16 − 5 = [ ]

(c)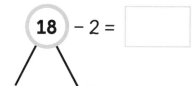

(d)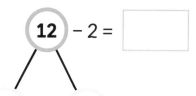

3 Subtract from 10, then fill in the blanks.

(a)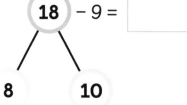

(b)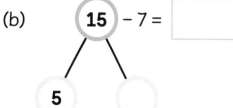

(c)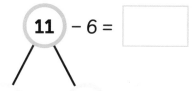

(d)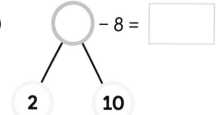

4 Subtract, then fill in the blanks.

(a)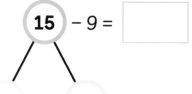

(b)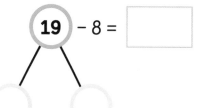

(c)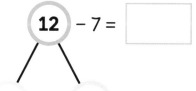

(d)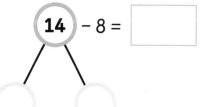

Families of addition and subtraction facts

Starter

I can tell an addition story using these numbers.

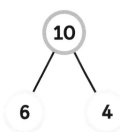

I can tell a subtraction story using these numbers.

. Can you tell more than one story with these numbers?

Example

I have 6 orange buttons and 4 yellow buttons.
6 + 4 = 10
I have 10 buttons in total.

morning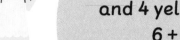

afternoon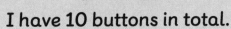

I can tell a different addition story. My mum's shop sold 4 drinks in the morning and 6 drinks in the afternoon.
4 + 6 = 10
Altogether, my mum's shop sold 10 drinks.

Is 6 + 4 the same as 4 + 6?

I can tell a subtraction story with the same numbers. We had 10 bananas. My family ate 4 bananas at breakfast.
10 − 4 = 6
There are 6 bananas left.

 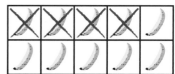

This is called a family of addition and subtraction facts.

Can you tell a different story using the same numbers?

6 + 4 = 10   10 − 4 = 6

4 + 6 = 10   10 − 6 = 4

Practice

1 Fill in the blanks to complete the families of addition and subtraction facts.

(a) 7 + 5 = ☐   12 − 7 = ☐

5 + ☐ = 12   12 − ☐ = 7

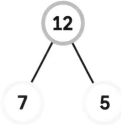

(b) 7 + 8 = ☐   15 − 7 = ☐

8 + ☐ = 15   15 − ☐ = 7

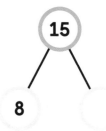

(c) 9 + 7 = ☐   16 − ☐ = ☐

☐ + ☐ = 16   ☐ − ☐ = 7

Counting and writing numbers to 40

Starter

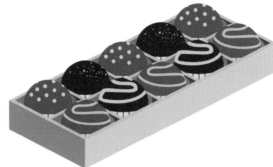

How many chocolates are there in total?

Example

10   20   21   22   23   24   25   26

Count the tens first and then count the ones.

20 + 6 = 26

2 0   +   6   =   2 6

20 means there are 2 tens.
6 means there are 6 ones.

1 Count the dots, then fill in the blanks.
The first one has been done for you.

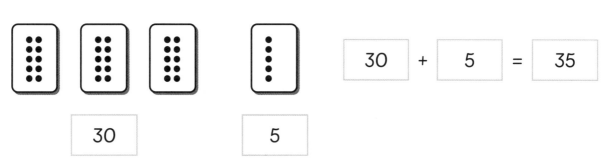

30   5

$30 + 5 = 35$

(a)

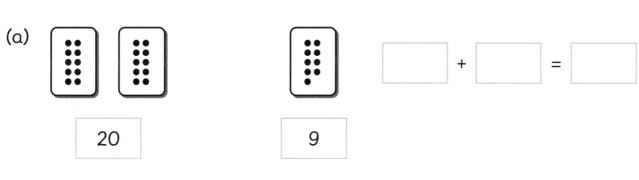

20   9

[ ] + [ ] = [ ]

(b)

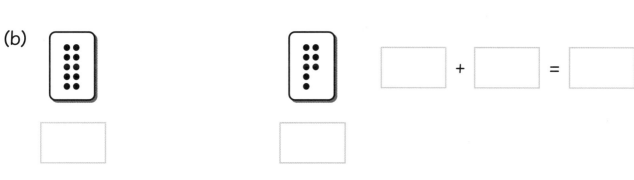

[ ] + [ ] = [ ]

(c)

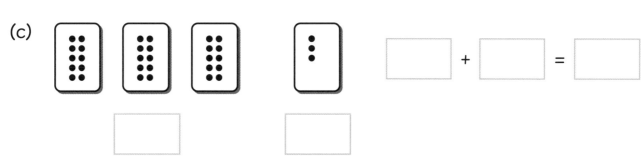

[ ] + [ ] = [ ]

2 Fill in the blanks and shade the ten frames to show the number.

(a) **3 0** + **3** = ☐

(b) **1 0** + **7** = ☐

(c) **2 0** + **9** = ☐

(d) **3 0** + **1** = ☐

3 Match.

    •   • 22

   •   • 25

     •   • 33

    •   • 40

     •   • 19

Counting in tens and ones

10 crayons   10 crayons

How many crayons are there?

Example

There are 2 packs of 10 crayons and 4 crayons on their own.

20   4

tens	ones
2	4

24 means 2 tens and 4 ones.

There are 24 crayons.

26

Practice

1 Fill in the blanks.

(a)

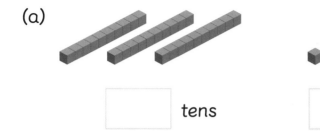

[ ] tens   [ ] ones

tens	ones
3	4

(b)

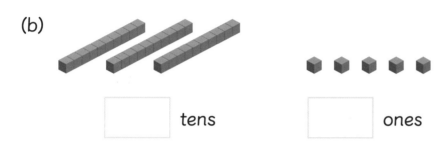

[ ] tens   [ ] ones

tens	ones

(c)

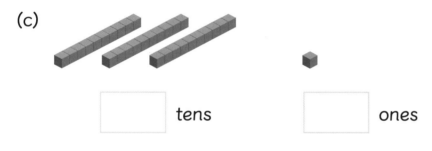

[ ] tens   [ ] ones

tens	ones

(d)

[ ] tens   [ ] ones

tens	ones

(e)

[ ] tens   [ ] ones

tens	ones

Counting to 100

Starter

10 Cards   10 Cards   10 Cards   10 Cards

How many cards are there altogether?

Example

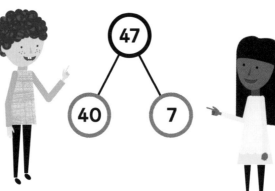

There are 4 packs of 10 cards and 7 cards on their own. There are 47 cards in total.

47
40   7

4 tens and 7 ones makes 47.

40   7

tens	ones
4	7

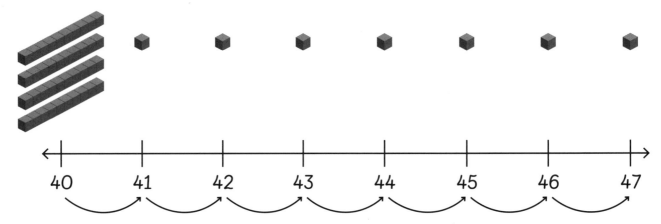

40   41   42   43   44   45   46   47

1 Count the stickers, fill in the blanks and trace the numbers.

⭐ stickers	1	ten 10
	___	tens 20
	___	tens 30
	___	tens 40
	___	tens 50
	___	tens 60
	___	tens 70
	___	tens 80
	___	tens 90
	___	tens 100

2 Count then write in numbers.

(a)

(b)

(c)

(d)

(e)

3 Complete the number bonds, fill in the blanks and match.

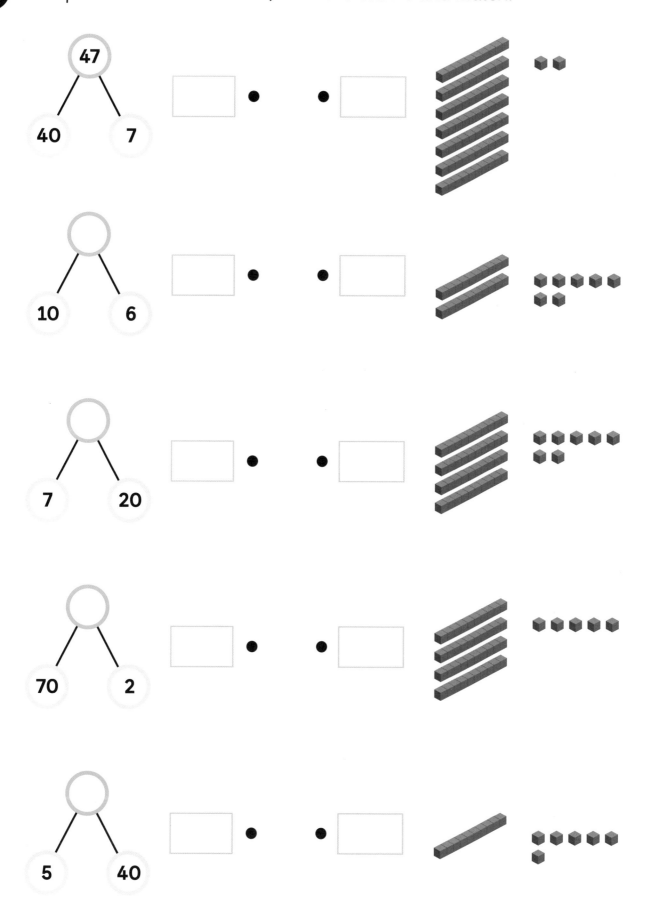

Comparing numbers

Starter

Are there equal numbers of each drink?

Example

tens	ones
5	8

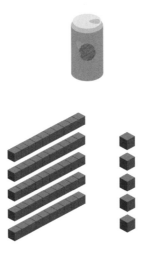

tens	ones
5	5

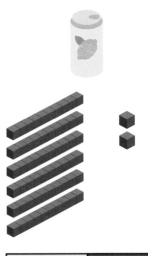

tens	ones
6	2

6 tens is more than 5 tens.
62 is more than 58 and 55.

There are more than .

There are more than .

62 is the greatest number.

First we compare the tens.

Both 55 and 58 have 5 tens. We compare the ones next.

5 ones is less than 8 ones.
55 is less than 58.

There are fewer than .

55 is the smallest number.

We can also check using a number line.

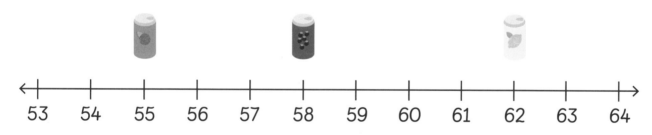

53 54 55 56 57 58 59 60 61 62 63 64

55
smallest → 58 62 greatest

62 58
55
greatest → smallest

1

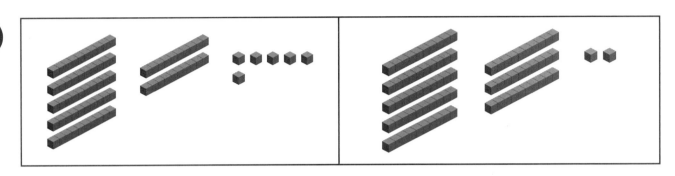

| | = | | tens | | ones | | = | | tens | | ones |

| | is more than | | . |

| | is less than | | . |

2

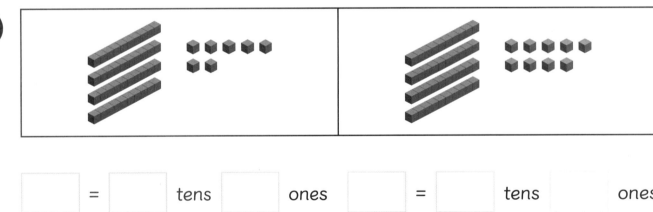

| | = | | tens | | ones | | = | | tens | | ones |

| | is more than | | . |

| | is less than | | . |

3 Circle the smallest number.

(a)

| 55 | 44 | 66 |

(b)

| 23 | 32 | 24 |

4 Circle the greatest number.

(a)

| 77 | 75 | 69 |

(b)

| 57 | 65 | 56 |

5 Arrange the numbers in order, starting with the smallest.

(a) 62, 41, 75   ☐ , ☐ , ☐

(b) 55, 65, 64   ☐ , ☐ , ☐

6 Arrange the numbers in order, starting with the greatest.

(a) 40, 53, 39   ☐ , ☐ , ☐

(b) 76, 66, 75   ☐ , ☐ , ☐

Making number patterns

2, 4, 6, 8, 10, 12
I can count forward
in twos. Each number
gets greater by two.

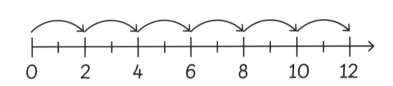

0   2   4   6   8   10   12

1 less 1 less 1 less 1 less

34	33	32	31	30	29	28

33, 32, 31, 30, 29
I can count backwards
in ones. Each number
gets smaller by one.

What are some other ways we know how to count?

36

I can count forward in fives. I can show it on a number line.

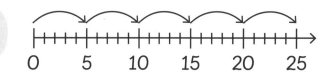

```
0    5   10   15   20   25
```

I can also show it on a number chart. This makes a pattern.

1	2	3	4	5	6	7	8	9	10
11	12	13	14	15	16	17	18	19	20
21	22	23	24	25	26	27	28	29	30

21	22	23	24	25	26	27	28	29	30
31	32	33	34	35	36	37	38	39	40
41	42	43	44	45	46	47	48	49	50
51	52	53	54	55	56	57	58	59	60

Counting in twos makes a pattern as well.

These are number patterns.

1 Fill in the blanks.

Count in twos and shade the numbers in yellow.

Count in fives and shade the numbers in blue.

The first row is done for you.

This is called a 100-square.

1	2	3	4	5	6	7	8	9	10
11	12	13		15	16	17	18	19	20
21	22	23	24	25	26	27	28	29	
31	32		34	35	36		38	39	40
41	42	43	44	45	46	47	48	49	50
51	52	53	54	55	56	57	58	59	60
61	62	63		65	66	67	68	69	70
71	72		74	75	76	77	78	79	80
81	82	83	84	85	86	87	88	89	90
91	92	93	94	95	96		98	99	100

2 What numbers are shaded in both yellow and blue?

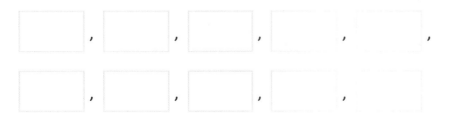

38

3 Fill in the blanks to complete the number patterns.

(a) 79, 80, 81, ☐ , 83, 84

(b) 20, 22, 24, 26, ☐ , 30

(c) ☐ , 97, 98, 99, 100

(d) 10, 15, 20, ☐ , 30, 35

(e) 76, 75, 74, ☐ , 72

(f) ☐ , 80, 82, 84

4 Fill in the blanks.

(a) 2 more than 17 is ☐ .

(b) 18 is 1 less than ☐ .

(c) 1 more than 89 is ☐ .

(d) ☐ is 5 more than 20.

(e) 1 less than 40 is ☐ .

Review and challenge

1 Fill in the blanks and match.

5 more than 15 [ ] . ●   ● fourteen

1 less than 12 [ ] . ●   ● twelve

1 more than 13 [ ] . ●   ● fifteen

5 more than 10 [ ] . ●   ● eighteen

1 less than 13 [ ] . ●   ● sixteen

2 less than 20 [ ] . ●   ● twenty

2 more than 14 [ ] . ●   ● seventeen

1 less than 20 [ ] . ●   ● eleven

1 more than 16 [ ] . ●   ● thirteen

1 more than 12 [ ] . ●   ● nineteen

2 Put the numbers in order from greatest to smallest.

(a)

| 12 | 14 | 11 |

☐ ☐ ☐

(b)

| 30 | 27 | 32 |

☐ ☐ ☐

(c)

| 60 | 54 | 53 |

☐ ☐ ☐

3 Put the numbers in order from smallest to greatest.

(a)

| 14 | 18 | 11 |

☐ ☐ ☐

(b)

| 32 | 27 | 19 |

☐ ☐ ☐

(c)

| 96 | 87 | 88 |

☐ ☐ ☐

4 Fill in the blanks.

(a) 53, 52, 51, ☐ , 49

(b) ☐ , ☐ , 17, 18

(c) ☐ , ☐ , 18, 17, 16

(d) ☐ , 97, 98, 99, ☐

(e) ☐ is 1 more than 49.

(f) ☐ is 1 less than 60.

5 Add by counting on.

1	2	3	4	5	6	7	8	9	10
11	12	13	14	15	16	17	18	19	20

(a) 2 + 8 =

(b) 9 + 5 =

(c) 16 + 3 =

(d) 2 + 17 =

6 Make 10 and add.

(a)

(b)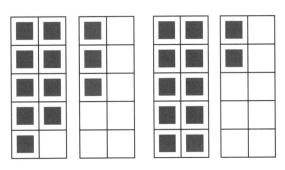

9 + 3 =

(c)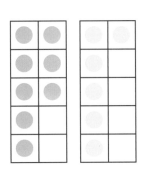

8 + =

7 Add the ones, then fill in the blanks.

(a)   (12) + 7 = ☐

  / \
10

(b)   4 + (15) = ☐

  / \
      10

8 Subtract by counting back. Use the number track to help you.

(a) 13 − 3 = ☐

5	6	7	8	9	10	11	12	13	14	15	16	17	18	19	20

(b) 15 − 8 = ☐

5	6	7	8	9	10	11	12	13	14	15	16	17	18	19	20

9 Subtract from the ones, then fill in the blanks.

(a)   (16) − 5 = ☐

  / \
10

(b)   (18) − 4 = ☐

  / \

10 Subtract from the tens, then fill in the blanks.

(a)   (12) − 6 = ☐

  / \
2

(b)   (14) − 9 = ☐

  / \

Fill in the blanks.

(a)

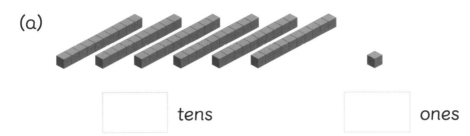

| | tens |

| | ones |

tens	ones

(b)

| | tens |

| | ones |

tens	ones

(c)

| | tens |

| | ones |

tens	ones

(d)

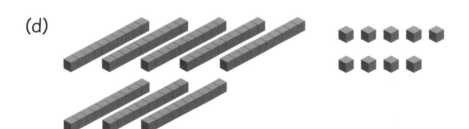

| | tens |

| | ones |

tens	ones

12 Complete the number bonds and match.

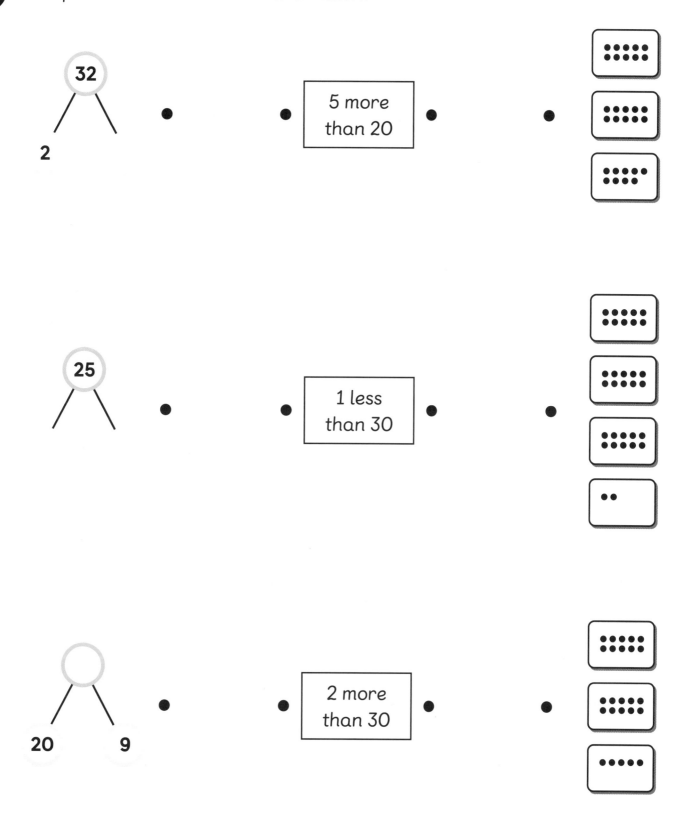

Answers

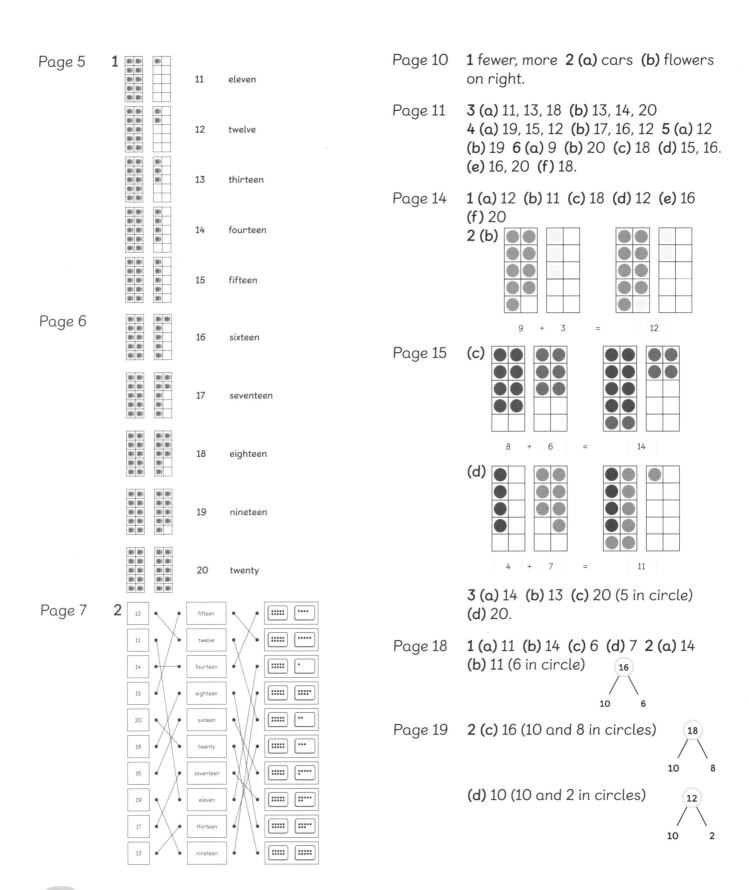

Page 5 **1**

11 eleven

12 twelve

13 thirteen

14 fourteen

15 fifteen

Page 6

16 sixteen

17 seventeen

18 eighteen

19 nineteen

20 twenty

Page 7 **2**

12 — fifteen

11 — twelve

14 — fourteen

15 — eighteen

20 — sixteen

18 — twenty

16 — seventeen

19 — eleven

17 — thirteen

13 — nineteen

Page 10 **1** fewer, more **2 (a)** cars **(b)** flowers on right.

Page 11 **3 (a)** 11, 13, 18 **(b)** 13, 14, 20
4 (a) 19, 15, 12 **(b)** 17, 16, 12 **5 (a)** 12
(b) 19 **6 (a)** 9 **(b)** 20 **(c)** 18 **(d)** 15, 16.
(e) 16, 20 **(f)** 18.

Page 14 **1 (a)** 12 **(b)** 11 **(c)** 18 **(d)** 12 **(e)** 16
(f) 20
2 (b)

9 + 3 = 12

Page 15 **(c)**

8 + 6 = 14

(d)

4 + 7 = 11

3 (a) 14 **(b)** 13 **(c)** 20 (5 in circle)
(d) 20.

Page 18 **1 (a)** 11 **(b)** 14 **(c)** 6 **(d)** 7 **2 (a)** 14
(b) 11 (6 in circle)

16
10   6

Page 19 **2 (c)** 16 (10 and 8 in circles)

18
10   8

(d) 10 (10 and 2 in circles)

12
10   2

3 (a) 9 **(b)** 8 (10 in circle)

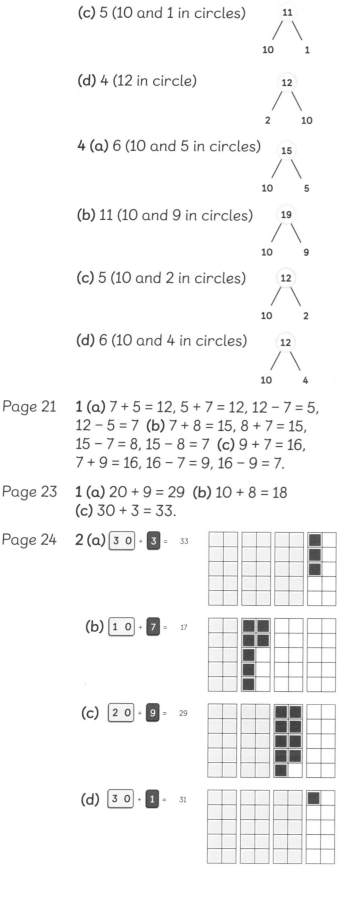

(c) 5 (10 and 1 in circles)

(d) 4 (12 in circle)

4 (a) 6 (10 and 5 in circles)

(b) 11 (10 and 9 in circles)

(c) 5 (10 and 2 in circles)

(d) 6 (10 and 4 in circles)

Page 21   **1 (a)** 7 + 5 = 12, 5 + 7 = 12, 12 − 7 = 5,
12 − 5 = 7 **(b)** 7 + 8 = 15, 8 + 7 = 15,
15 − 7 = 8, 15 − 8 = 7 **(c)** 9 + 7 = 16,
7 + 9 = 16, 16 − 7 = 9, 16 − 9 = 7.

Page 23   **1 (a)** 20 + 9 = 29 **(b)** 10 + 8 = 18
(c) 30 + 3 = 33.

Page 24   **2 (a)** 3 0 + 3 = 33

(b) 1 0 + 7 = 17

(c) 2 0 + 9 = 29

(d) 3 0 + 1 = 31

Page 25   **3**

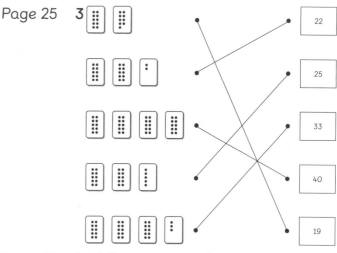

Page 27   **1 (a)** 3 tens 4 ones **(b)** 3 tens, 5 ones
(c) 3 tens, 1 one **(d)** 2 tens, 8 ones
(e) 4 tens, 0 ones.

Page 29   **1** 1 ten, 2 tens, 3 tens, 4 tens, 5 tens,
6 tens, 7 tens, 8 tens, 9 tens, 10 tens.

Page 30   **2 (a)** 19 **(b)** 22 **(c)** 100 **(d)** 97 **(e)** 50

Page 31   **3**

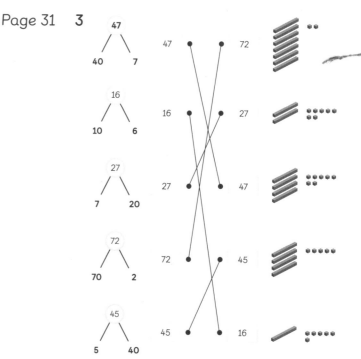

Page 34   **1** 76 = 7 tens 6 ones, 82 = 8 tens 2 ones,
82 is more than 76, 76 is less than 82.
2 47 = 4 tens 7 ones, 49 = 4 tens 9 ones,
49 is more than 47, 47 is less than 49.

Page 35   **3 (a)** 44 **(b)** 23 **4 (a)** 77 **(b)** 65 **5 (a)** 41,
62, 75 **(b)** 55, 64, 65 **6 (a)** 53, 40, 39
(b) 76, 75, 66.

Answers continued

Page 38

1

1	2	3	4	5	6	7	8	9	10
11	12	13	(14)	15	16	17	18	19	20
21	22	23	24	25	26	27	28	29	(30)
31	32	(33)	34	35	36	(37)	38	39	40
41	42	43	44	45	46	47	48	49	50
51	52	53	54	55	56	57	58	59	60
61	62	63	(64)	65	66	67	68	69	70
71	72	(73)	74	75	76	77	78	79	80
81	82	83	84	85	86	87	88	89	90
91	92	93	94	95	96	(97)	98	99	100

2 10, 20, 30, 40, 50, 60, 70, 80, 90, 100.

Page 39 **3 (a)** 82 **(b)** 28 **(c)** 96 **(d)** 25 **(e)** 73 **(f)** 78 **4 (a)** 19 **(b)** 19 **(c)** 90 **(d)** 25 **(e)** 39.

Page 40 **1**

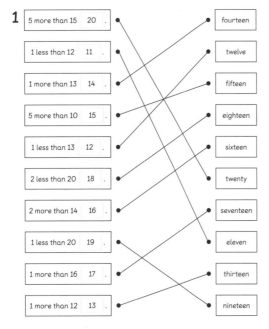

Page 41 **2 (a)** 14, 12, 11 **(b)** 32, 30, 27 **(c)** 60, 54, 53 **3 (a)** 11, 14, 18 **(b)** 19, 27, 32 **(c)** 87, 88, 96 **4 (a)** 50 **(b)** 15, 16 **(c)** 20, 19 **(d)** 96, 100 **(e)** 50 **(f)** 59.

Page 42 **5 (a)** 10 **(b)** 14 **(c)** 19 **(d)** 19 **6 (a)** 10 + 2 = 12 **(b)** 9 + 3 = 12 **(c)** 8 + 6 = 14.

Page 43 **7 (a)** (12) + 7 = 19, 10 and 2 **(b)** 4 + (15) = 19, 5 and 10

8 (a) 10 **(b)** 7

9 (a) (16) − 5 = 11, 10 and 6 **(b)** (18) − 4 = 14, 10 and 8

10 (a) (12) − 6 = 6, 2 and 10 **(b)** (14) − 9 = 5, 10 and 4

Page 44 **11 (a)** 6 tens, 1 one **(b)** 2 tens, 9 ones **(c)** 4 tens, 0 ones **(d)** 8 tens, 9 ones.

Page 45 **12**

48